THE LAST LIGHT OF DAY

THE LAST LIGHT OF DAY

Landscape of the Delaware River

PHOTOGRAPHS BY DOUGLAS PETERSEN

Introduction by Cynthia Poten

DEERFIELD EDITIONS · ANDOVER · NEW JERSEY

Photographs copyright © 1997 by Douglas Petersen
Text introduction copyright © 1997 by Cynthia Poten
ISBN: 0-9655747-0-9

For their advice and encouragement I wish to acknowledge Michael and Meredith Bzdak, Stephen Rosenberg and Fran Kaufman and Cynthia Poten.   D. P.

Deerfield Editions
163 Andover Mohawk Road
Andover, New Jersey 07821
Tel/Fax 201-786-6939

FRONTISPIECE: *High Water in Springtime, Sandts Eddy*

For my wife, Constance Petersen

Delaware Water Gap from Columbia

THE PEOPLE'S RIVER
by Cynthia Poten

THE DELAWARE IS AN INTIMATE RIVER, meandering through a landscape that enfolds and encloses. Even its cliffs invite contact, offering faces covered with wildflowers and ledges for climbing and sitting. Breathtaking views from river's heights seem the counterpoint to a predominant mood of tranquility. Hawks Nest Mountain, north of Port Jervis, has a spectacular vista. On both sides of the river, 250-foot sheer cliffs look down upon a leisurely meander, and the rapids below, which can be tricky in high water, are reduced to glistening ripples. The views from the mountains of the Delaware Water Gap have inspired some of the most serene visions in American landscape painting.

Until it reaches Trenton, the Delaware is narrow and often shallow. The bridges that span this 200-mile stretch are modest in scale and seem diminutive when compared with the monumental and lofty bridges of the Hudson. Yet they have their own elegance. One of the most beautiful, designed by Roebling and a near miniature of the Brooklyn Bridge, can be found at Reigelsville, Pennsylvania. The Delaware's bridges are vital links between the towns that face one another across the river, and pedestrian use of them is considerable.

During dry weather and low flows, the riverbed's edges become cobbled paths. There are places where one can wade to the other side in a few minutes. There are banks with flat, broad sheets of rock, some extending almost to the midpoint of the river. There are also abundant pools, the deepest being at Narrowsburg, New York, south of the bridge there. By day these pools attract fishermen. Towards evening, the wildlife comes out. In the Upper Delaware I've seen a black bear come to the river at dusk, swim clear to the other side of Knights Eddy and then swim back again, getting out of the water just about where it got in.

The Delaware is a place to be in and on. Put in anywhere on the non-tidal river in midsummer and you'll drift by stands of canary grass, mullein, purple loosestrife, St. Johnswort or yarrow. Occasionally you'll see patches of cardinal flowers, blue vervain and wild forget-me-nots. Scores of wooded islands have been created by the river, affording quiet, shaded channels and remote campsites. The river's rapids are relatively tame. Dramatic exceptions provide an exciting contrast to the generally gentle demeanor of the current. Foul Rift, south of Belvidere, New Jersey, where the river drops twenty-two feet in a half mile, is the most severe rapids. The river's highest standing waves are those at Mongaup Falls, where a chute created by a boulder ledge funnels the water into three-foot haystacks.

The river's original habitat was dense forest, and trees again dominate the shoreline. The floodplain's fields and hedgerows, towns and factories, generating stations and railroad tracks, are enfolded in stands of sycamore, willow, beech, birch and maple; white hemlock woods cover rocky slopes. Woodlands are the warp and weft of the valley's fabric, holding its soils in place, providing havens for wildlife, and crucial habitat for the Americas' migrating song birds.

Before the Europeans assumed dominion over its forests, flow and identity, the Delaware had the same name as its native inhabitants—the Lenapi. While the word Lenape means *the people*, it's unlikely that the Lenni Lenape gave the river their name to mark ownership. Possessing elements of the natural world is an alien idea to Native American peoples, whose spiritual traditions imply that the naming had a deeper meaning. The Cherokees, another Eastern woodlands tribe, called rivers *long human beings*. Naming the river after themselves, calling it *the people's river*, suggests to me that the Lenape felt an inextricable link between human beings and the Being of the River.

This watery Being, this immense yet subtle force who never stops moving, whom we can see but in part and in passing, does have something in common with us. For rivers and human beings can, by virtue of their innate powers, move hundreds of miles over the land, inch by inch over rock and soil, from the shaded woodlands of headwater streams to the shimmering marshlands of a luminous bay. The Lenape's summer trek to the Atlantic ocean embodied this similitude, the sound of moccasined footsteps a rhythmic echo of the river's song as it flows inexorably downstream, over boulders and cobbles, through shallows and pools, into eddies and backwaters.

Technological progress has obscured the essential unity of human life and the natural environment evident in this annual walk to the sea. Nevertheless this unity, tangible as light, can still be experienced in the environs of the Lenape's river. Observed from the shore, from bridges, hilltops or canoe, its landscapes nourish a sense of being with an immanent presence; it becomes possible to enter the river's realm of timelessness and transcendence.

This spiritual reckoning is a personal affair in our culture, a private knowledge, unrecognized in and seemingly irrelevant to public life. Our common knowledge remains a matter of science and the written word. For the Delaware, the body of facts and figures is extensive. We have located its headwaters, wetlands, springs, its marshes and limestone fens; mapped its tributaries; inventoried its aquatic life; surveyed its groundwater; identified its flora and fauna, and recorded its geology. We know where the fresh water, some of which flows all the way from the Catskill Mountains, meets the salt water brought in on the tides. We know the state of its economy, its environmental problems and recreational and real estate values. We know its natural and unnatural history, a tale told in miniature by its past and current name. For the Delaware was named after a Lord, emblem of the Europeans who led the conquest of the river's native people and lands.

Perhaps its Native American name has in some way shaped the particular destiny shared by the Delaware and its European descendants. From an economic and political perspective, the Delaware is notably a people's river. It serves more people relative to its size than any other river in the United States, providing drinking water to over seven percent of the nation's population. The world's first experiment in government by the people was born along the banks of the river in Philadelphia, where the Declaration of Independence and the Constitution were drafted. The people of the Delaware River watershed waged the longest environmental battle in the history of the country, trying to stop a diversion of water that was destined to cool nuclear generators and supply water for new homes. The battle was ultimately lost, and thousands of acres of some of the richest farmland in North America are now covered with housing developments. But an earlier people's effort was successful—the one to stop a massive dam on the river above the Water Gap. The Delaware is the only major river east of the Mississippi without a dam on its main stem. Since 1990, the river and its watershed has had a people's network of volunteers who monitor water quality, restore streambanks and take action at the local level to assure the protection of their home waters.

Civilization arose in river valleys. While indigenous people knew their life depended on water and offered ceremonial prayers of thanks in return for the river's gifts, our way was to harness its power. We over-harvested its fish, and forced it to swallow our waste and cool our machines. Our way reversed the paradigm—today the fate of rivers depends on people. Yet, as our daily life becomes ever more confined within constructs of the human mind, ever more accelerated by electricity and engines, the undammed flow of the Delaware reminds us that the natural world has a different pace. Even now, tamed, trashed and polluted as it has been, the Delaware sings of serenity and exhilaration, of the ephemeral and the eternal.

Cynthia Poten served as the Delaware Riverkeeper from 1988–1996 and is a founder of the Delaware Riverkeeper Network, located in Washington Crossing, PA.

Reigelsville, The Last Light of Day

Bull's Island, Stockton

Portland with Delaware Water Gap Beyond

A Bend in the River North of Riverton

High Water, Yardley River Access

The Pequest Joins the Delaware at Belvidere

View North from Belvidere

Hawks Nest in Winter

Route 80 at Delaware Water Gap

Church in Fog, Portland

The Old Delaware Canal

The Delaware Canal at Raubsville

Fry's Run, Late Autumn

Hugh Moore Park, Easton

Two Fishermen, Tinicum Launch

The Forks of the Delaware

Phillipsburg with Northampton Street Bridge

Easton, An Early Summer Evening

Philadelphia Skyline from Camden

Washington Crossing State Park

Springtime Near Lumberville

Delaware River at Bushkill

Tocks Island on a Summer Evening

Pennington Island from Tinicum Access

A Warm November Afternoon Near Reigelsville

One thousand copies of this book were printed on Monadnock Dulcet 80# cover,
of which twenty-five have been reserved for a special edition.
The photographs were reproduced as 300-line tritones and printed at
The Stinehour Press, Lunenburg, Vermont.
Binding by Roswell Bookbinding, Phoenix, Arizona.
Design and typography by Dean Bornstein.